T0067181

THE DEVIL
IN THE KITCHEN

How to Overcome the Demons
That Drive You to the Kitchen

(Confessions of an X victim of eating disorders)

Laurie Poimboeuf

BALBOA.
PRESS
A DIVISION OF HAY HOUSE

Copyright © 2017 Laurie Poimboeuf.

All rights reserved. No part of this book may be used or reproduced by any means, graphic, electronic, or mechanical, including photocopying, recording, taping or by any information storage retrieval system without the written permission of the author except in the case of brief quotations embodied in critical articles and reviews.

Balboa Press books may be ordered through booksellers or by contacting:

Balboa Press
A Division of Hay House
1663 Liberty Drive
Bloomington, IN 47403
www.balboapress.com
1 (877) 407-4847

Because of the dynamic nature of the Internet, any web addresses or links contained in this book may have changed since publication and may no longer be valid. The views expressed in this work are solely those of the author and do not necessarily reflect the views of the publisher, and the publisher hereby disclaims any responsibility for them.

The author of this book does not dispense medical advice or prescribe the use of any technique as a form of treatment for physical, emotional, or medical problems without the advice of a physician, either directly or indirectly. The intent of the author is only to offer information of a general nature to help you in your quest for emotional and spiritual well-being. In the event you use any of the information in this book for yourself, which is your constitutional right, the author and the publisher assume no responsibility for your actions.

This book is a work of non-fiction. Unless otherwise noted, the author and the publisher make no explicit guarantees as to the accuracy of the information contained in this book and in some cases, names of people and places have been altered to protect their privacy.

Any people depicted in stock imagery provided by Thinkstock are models, and such images are being used for illustrative purposes only.
Certain stock imagery © Thinkstock.

Print information available on the last page.

ISBN: 978-1-5043-8612-8 (sc)
ISBN: 978-1-5043-8613-5 (e)

Library of Congress Control Number: 2017912740

Balboa Press rev. date: 08/26/2017

CONTENTS

PROLOGUE

It's hard for someone who has never had a compulsive behavior to understand what it's like. Most of the time, it's hard for the person with that behavior to recognize the fact that they have a problem.

There is always a psychological "benefit" to that compulsive behavior, meaning that it fills some kind of psychological need. Some compulsive behaviors can have physical "benefits "as well. An example would be someone who has an addiction to drugs. They may be unhappy, so they take drugs to make them feel better emotionally, at the same time they get a physical sense of well being too. Eventually this can become a psychological, as well as a physical addiction. An alcoholic would be another example. They have an emotional need that is being taken care of by the alcohol, but they also get a physical sense of well being, which will lead to a chemical addiction. A drug addict or an alcoholic cannot stop their addiction without experiencing some physical withdrawals as well. These two addictions are very difficult to overcome because they have both a psychological addiction and a physical addiction to overcome. This usually requires medical supervision because the physical addiction to the drug or alcohol can be life threatening. Drug and Alcohol abuse has become an epidemic in society today.

There are several other epidemics occurring in society today.

Obesity is one of them. Nationally nearly 38% of adults are obese, and nearly 8% are extremely obese. While we have the most overweight citizens in terms of numbers, a few other countries actually have higher rates of obesity. Obesity without some underlying physical problem is an eating disorder.

One of the most common eating disorders is binge eating disorder. Binge eating disorder affects an estimated 2.8 million people in the United States according to a national survey. BED is where people consume excessive amounts of food in a single sitting. Unlike bulimia, a person with BED does not throw up. BED can lead to obesity, but you can have obesity without having BED.

On the other end of the spectrum, 1 in 200 American Women suffers from anorexia, and 3 in 100 American Women suffer from bulimia. "The National Association of Anorexia Nervosa and Associated Disorders states that approximately eight million people in the U.S. have anorexia nervosa, bulimia, and related eating disorders. Eight million people represent about three percent (3%) of the total population. The prevalence of eating disorders is highest in Western countries, but it appears to be increasing in non-Western countries.

It is really difficult in today's society to know what a healthy body and healthy weight should look like. We are bombarded by advertisements that show tall, glamorous, and extremely thin models advertising everything from clothing, underwear, and makeup, to alcohol, cars, and motorcycles. They are plastered across billboards, television, magazines, and advertisements that pop up on your email site, and social media. They all look very beautiful and perfect, and you wonder how they do it. And it's not just women. There are handsome men, with rippling muscles, and perfect six pack abs standing around in their underwear, like it was some kind of suit, on page after page of magazines.

Some of these people have great metabolisms, work out, and eat healthy. Some of them literally starve themselves to look that way. You have to be pretty tall to be a model, which contributes to a faster metabolic rate. There is also a lot of photo shop going on, as well.

This is their job. That's how they make their money. They are under a tremendous amount of pressure to maintain, or lose weight just to be able to have an income. I don't know about you, but that kind of pressure is not for me. At least you and I can gain a pound, and still get a paycheck.

At the same time that we are getting to see all these beautiful people, we are also getting to see advertisements of juicy hamburgers and fries, telling us to supersize. Or pizza and spaghetti along with mouth watering desserts. It's enough to make anyone crazy.

So many people feel pressured to look like those models, and at the same time they are being enticed to eat all those fattening foods. Two important factors to remember: Your body is not "Who You Are", and food is meant to sustain life, not to become your life.

It took me a very long time to learn those two little phrases because I was one of the above statistics. I had bulimia. I didn't even wait for it to become popular. I started back in the 80's when I finally got tired of dieting to get small, then gaining it back the minute I got off the diet. I wasn't even that big, but I was proactively determined not to get anywhere close to being big.

I'm sharing my story today because I'm hoping it will help other people. If you have an eating disorder, know someone with an eating disorder, or have problems with weight, I think hearing my story might shed some light on why you or your loved one, have this unhealthy relationship with food. Once you understand why, it will be much easier to face the challenge head on, and conquer this problem once and for all. The biggest challenge with Eating Disorders is that abstinence is not an option. Unlike Alcohol and Drugs, you can't just abstain from eating. In fact that is one of the Eating Disorders, Anorexia. You are going to have to reprogram your relationship with food, understand how you got that programming in the first place, as well as break bad eating habits.

CHAPTER 1

❋

THE SHAME OF IT ALL....

*T*he first thing I would like to make clear is that it took a very long time to admit to the fact that I had an eating disorder. Many years had to pass even after my healing of this self induced disease before I could tell anyone my story. I felt that people would see me as a failure, or weak. Today I feel very different about that time of my life. Sometimes the worst things that happen in your life can end up being the greatest blessings. A bad experience can end up being a good thing as long as you learn something from it. It can end up an even better thing if you use your knowledge to better your life. Ultimately it can even become a wonderful experience if you use the same knowledge to help other people. That's why I have chosen to share my story with you.

My eating disorder was Bulimia, but I truly believe that all eating disorders are basically the same. Whether you are Bulimic, Anorexic, or significantly overweight (without underlying physical reasons for the weight), you have an unhealthy relationship to food. As a result, you also have an unhealthy self image. Your, self image is not healthy because you are either overweight, or you think you are overweight, or you are afraid of becoming overweight. Whatever

1

the reason, it's not a healthy circumstance. You've also forgotten that your "self" is not just the physical body that you see in the mirror. In fact the physical body is more like a vehicle for the self, a way to access the self in the physical world. There is nothing wrong with having a nice looking vehicle, as long as you realize that the main purpose of that vehicle is to enable you to function in the world. The better care you take of your vehicle, the better it will serve you to function in this world. Taking care of your vehicle also leads to a more attractive vehicle. The important thing to remember is that is not WHO YOU REALLY ARE.

Another thing that I have learned through my experience is that most disorders, or obsessive behaviors, are a result of an unresolved issue or hurt, which you have experienced in your life. You may not remember the experience, but it happened most definitely. Surely you can't believe that you were just born with an obsessive behavior. You didn't just pop out of your mother with a desire to eat unrealistic amounts of food, or gamble away all your money, or stay high all day long. These obsessions are just the way you deal with the pain that resulted from your bad experience. They give you some kind of relief or comfort from the pain that won't go away. This is the problem; it's about the same as putting a band aid on the spot where a sword just pierce your heart. It might catch a little of the bleeding, but the situation will ultimately get worse unless something else is done.

The Real Problem is that you already have a bad self image, and although this obsession gives you some temporary relief, the obsession itself causes you to have a worse self image. It's a snowball effect. You know that it's not normal to eat mass quantities of food, or have a new sexual conquest every week, or spend every dime at a casino, so you come to the realization that you have a major issue.

You add this issue to all the other things you hate about yourself, and the problem gets worse and worse as you go along. It needs to be stopped, but by this time you have such a distorted image of reality you can't think straight enough to remember what normal looks like. It's difficult to admit you have this problem out loud because it makes you hate yourself even more, so pretending it doesn't exist, and lying to yourself is your new daily routine.

No one can talk to you about it because it would devastate you if someone else knew who you really were. If anyone dares to bring it up you get violently argumentative in order to dissuade the person from raising the issue again. That's what I did anyway. I would get so loud and argumentative every time my Mom tried to talk to me about it that she was afraid to raise the subject. I think she was actually afraid that I would hurt myself if she kept talking about it, but she was also afraid I would die if I kept up the Bulimia.

So what do you do in this circumstance? How do you deal with a person who can't admit that they have a problem because they hate themselves for having it in the first place? They are ashamed and don't want you to see them for who they really are, because they just couldn't stand to have one more person be disappointed in them like they are in themselves.

I don't claim to be an expert on the subject. I just know that I was the person with that kind of problem. I had Bulimia and I hated myself for having it. I was in a vicious cycle, and couldn't get out. Today I am completely healed of that, and I am even better off because I had the Bulimia. I learned to understand and love myself in ways that would not have been possible if I had not had the Bulimia. I learned to dig deep and understand why I do the things I do, because of that experience.

I overcame this obsession without going to a clinic, or seeing a physician. I'm not saying you shouldn't go to a clinic or see a doctor about this problem. I'm just letting you know that I didn't end up doing that. Maybe the person who walked me through the ultimate healing process had seen a psychiatrist, and I was able to benefit from her experience. That's the reason I am writing this book. I hope that someone else can hear my story and either help themselves, or help someone they love, to overcome their problem and end up even stronger and better than before. There is a saying that goes like this, "What does not kill us makes us stronger"; I think it was Friedrich Nietzsche. That was definitely what happened to me. Today I look at my Bulimia as one of the best things that happened to me. Not only do I understand myself and dig much deeper to understand who I am, I also learn a great deal about nutrition and how to eat healthy. That doesn't mean I don't have a burger and fries every now and then, but I consistently eat good on a regular basis. I am so happy that I had this experience at a young age because I have been eating healthy for a very long time.

So let's get started. I plan to tell you my story as best as I can remember it. It might be a little painful to me, and maybe even to some of the people that caused my pain as a child, but it's necessary. If sharing this can help someone else, then so be it.

CHAPTER 2

※

MAKING CHANGES.........

My freshman year in college had just started. I was in my first semester, and had done quite well for myself. My mom had insisted that I go out for a sorority, which I didn't really want to do. My sister had done so the year she went to college, and had not gotten a bid to the sorority she wanted to join. I thought that was so mean, so I wasn't really that interested, but my Mom pushed me to do it. She said that I needed to be a "Joiner" whatever that means, so I went through "Rush". To my great joy and relief, I got accepted to a decent sorority. I had just finished my first semester and it was Christmas break. I had some time off, so I wanted to make it a productive time. I had packed on a few pounds since the summer by eating too many burgers and fries, so I decided to go on a diet. I had also been smoking cigarettes off and on for years and I really wanted to quit, so that was another goal I made. My final goal was really the hardest one, and that was to stop using nose spray. I know that sounds crazy, but I had gotten addicted to that nose spray some time during high school when I had a cold, and couldn't go without it. The problem is that the more you use it the less it works, so I had to use that nose spray all the time. I had to carry it in my purse if I went out or I couldn't breathe. Of all my goals, this was going to be the hardest because I would get miserable when the nose spray wore off and my nose would just basically close up. The only way I could break the habit was to stop using it cold turkey. That meant I would have to breathe through my mouth until the rebound effect of the spray wore off. That could be days or weeks, but hopefully it would be ok by the time I went back to school.

I decided to quit smoking the same way, "Cold Turkey". Since I would only be able to breathe through my mouth, quitting smoking wouldn't be so hard. My weight loss plan was to follow a diet my mother knew about. It had a set eating plan, and told you exactly what to eat, so you couldn't go wrong.

So here I was making myself miserable over Christmas break, but making all kinds of positive changes for the New Year. I know this is hard to believe, but the diet and the quitting smoking were really pretty easy, but getting off the nose spray was rough. If you can only breathe through your mouth, you are not as inclined to be putting stuff in it. I had to eat in between breaths, and there was no way I was going to put a cigarette in my mouth when oxygen was so hard to come by. I ended up sleeping in a recliner in the living room because I was too stuffed up to lay down flat. It's a horrible feeling to have your nose stopped up, and because I had used that spray for several years, it took almost two weeks for my nose to get back to normal. By the time I went back to school, I had accomplished my goals. I had stopped using the nose spray, quit smoking, and had lost weight. I can't remember what I weighed when I started, or what I weighed when I finished, but I know it was above 100 pounds, because I was later to start dropping my weight below the 100 marker. I do however know that it was a noticeable difference because when I went back to the sorority house, people were amazed at the difference in my weight. I must have really packed on some pounds that first semester for them to have noticed it to such a degree.

I was thrilled at the response to my new weight and was determined to stay small. I took extra PE classes since there was no extra charge for classes because I was at full time student. It was great because it made me work out. I actually started liking it so much that I joined a Gym. I worked out every day, and sometimes twice a day. I was doing great, but there was only one problem. I was hanging around a bunch of college kids who thought that pizza, burgers and fries was a balanced diet. I ate pretty decent when I was home, but since I was in a sorority, I had to be on campus for meetings and other events more than just going to class. I ended up eating away from the house quite a bit, and even though I worked out hard, the weight started to creep back. There was always someone eating some kind of junk at the sorority house, and it was impossible to get away from the temptation.

I was so upset that I was starting to gain my weight back. I had worked so hard to get it off and I was really getting a lot of attention now, especially from guys. It was a blast, and I wasn't going to let myself gain the weight back. I had just really started to feel good about myself. Except for the last two years in High School, I had not felt that way for a very long time. I was so grateful that my parents had moved to Lafayette and I got to attend Cathedral Carmel High School. I loved my last two years of High School there, and I had hated school since about the sixth grade before that. Now I was in college, and it looked like it was going to be a continuation of my Junior and Senior years in High School. This was how it was supposed to be. High School and College were supposed to be fun, and nothing was going to stop me now.

I had recently heard about how some models would throw up their food after they eat in order to stay slim. I figured that if it was good enough for a model, it was good enough for me. The smart thing would have been to just start eating healthy, but that thought didn't even enter my head. I really didn't know what eating healthy was. If it was anything like dieting, you could have it. I wasn't interested. When I had dieted, the food was boring and I always felt hungry. I wasn't planning to go through that again. So there I was. My plan to keep slim and popular was to throw up my meals.

When I first started throwing up I had to stick my finger down my throat to do it. This was not very pleasant, but neither was being chunky and unpopular. What I failed to realize is that in my younger years of being unpopular, I was not overweight. It was a self esteem issue which I will explain the details of later. My problem was that I thought of myself as a body. As long as my body looked good, I figured that I would be popular. That was not really a way off theory for the age I was. In High school and College image is everything. I think most people my age felt the same way as I did. It is somewhat unusual for a person to be enlightened enough at age nineteen to realize their value outside of their looks. So I kept up the game. Eat a meal, then run to the bathroom and throw up. The problem was that I was so good at throwing up, I would be hungry again right after. I would get so hungry that I had to eat, and then I would get worried that I would gain weight, so I would throw up again. It became a miserable and vicious cycle. Eat, throw up, eat, and throw up. I was always eating something and then running to the bathroom.

Something else started happening during that time. I would get so hungry a short while after throwing up that when I finally ate again, I would feel relieved. I started associating eating with relief. The throwing up caused stress, so I would feel relief when I ate. Later when I would have stress for other reasons, eating would help relieve it. Eating food started to become how I would handle stress. I would eat if I got stressed out, but then after I ate I would worry that I was going to gain weight, so I would throw up. Once I threw up, I was hungry again which caused me stress, so I ate again. My whole life became about eating and throwing up. I did go to school, work, exercise and party, but during all that I was throwing up.

I started to worry that people might suspect what I was doing. My Mom had started to look at me in a strange way. She took me to the doctor to have my Thyroid checked out, or so she said. What I later found out is she suspected what I was doing and she was trying to make sure I wasn't hurting myself. She would try to talk to me about it and I would blow up. I couldn't bear the thought of someone knowing what I was doing. I wanted people to like me and I just knew they would hate me, and pick on me if they knew what I was doing. I couldn't even remember what it was like to not be throwing up. I don't know how I kept my secret from so many of my friends. I think maybe a lot of them could eat a decent amount of food and not gain weight, so they believed that I could too. I also worked out all the time and they just figured that I burned off a lot of food, so I could eat a lot. I think most of the people who knew about my problem were my family members, and they didn't know what to do about it because of the way I would act if they tried to bring it up. I even had guys I dated who didn't know about my disorder.

It was my deep dark secret that I could never let anyone know about. I hated myself and I felt so ashamed. I didn't know how to stop. I know that sounds strange to someone who has never experienced this, but it's true. It's an addiction, a true addiction. I was addicted to that behavior. I felt relief when I ate, and I felt relief when I threw up. I didn't know how to exist beyond that relationship with food. As I sit here and write this, I am amazed at how long I was bulimic. I used to think it was about a year or so, but when I actually calculate how long it lasted, it was at least four years. I can't believe I survived that long with that disease. I guess the binging helped me because I would eat so much that I couldn't throw it all up and I guess I got some nutrition from that. I eventually got down to 94 pounds and I am 5' 3". I looked terrible at that weight because I was too thin, but I would have been happier being thinner. Because I am not very tall a few pounds either way makes a difference on me. I was later 110 pounds, a personal trainer, and I looked healthy, even by my mother's standards. At 94 pounds I looked sickly, but I was luckier than most because I have since then seen pictures of girls who look like a walking skeleton.

To the rest of the world I looked like a very thin, muscular girl. I made good grades in school, worked part time, and had fun partying with my friends. I looked like a normal college girl, but deep down inside I was so unhappy. It was like the world saw one side of me, but I knew the real truth. When I was with my friends, I could forget my problem. Even when I was in the bathroom throwing up,

I would act like it wasn't happening, as long as I was out with other people. It was when I was alone sometimes, and I couldn't hide away from my thoughts that I was in anguish. There were times when I just couldn't shut out my disgust for myself. I would almost feel a physical pain because of the life I was leading. That was some of the darkest times of my life.

CHAPTER 3

TURNING THE CORNER.......

J don't know what would have happened to me if I had kept on with the Bulimia. I wonder if I would even be alive today. I'm 55 years old, and I think about all the things I have gone through in my life, and I know I could never have made it in the fragile state that I was back then.

I continued on my destructive path through the end on my college years, and into my first job out of college. I guess it was a little less than a year since I graduated college that someone was finally able to reach me. I really wanted to stop what I was doing, but since I couldn't talk about what was going on, no one could help me. My brother came up with a plan.

He decided to send me a letter, since I would freak out whenever someone tried to talk about it. He was the typical big brother when I was growing up. Always teasing, picking, and basically making my life and my sister's life miserable. I was convinced he hated my guts. One time in college, he was trying to put together a trip to Cozumel, and he needed a certain number of people to get a discounted trip. I was so surprised that he asked me, but I knew it was because of the discount. On the trip, a girl who was a friend of his had an accident on a moped. The next day he asked me if I wanted to ride the moped, and I said no, because I thought he wanted me to get in an accident. I really believed he wanted to get rid of me. I only tell you this story so you can see how convinced I was that my brother despised me.

I got a letter from him at the apartment I lived in near campus. I started reading the letter, and I couldn't believe what it said. He told me that he loved me, and believed in me, and that he and I were the strongest in the family. Imagine my surprise that my brother, who I thought hated me, actually loved me, and believed in me. He said that he would be there for me, and help me get over this terrible thing I was doing to myself. I can't believe now, that I didn't keep the letter. After a few years I got rid of it because I didn't want anyone to know about my past. I wish now, that I had kept it, especially since I'm writing this book. I think it would be beneficial for those who have love ones suffering from this "dysfunction" to know how to approach them. I think writing a letter is good, because the person doesn't have to see your face. It's a detached type of acknowledgement of the issue, and it gives them time to process that someone knows. It's also important to let them know that you love them, and will help them through the problem. My brother sent along a book. I thought it was strange because the book appeared to be about sales, and at the time, I had no intention of becoming a sales person. The book was written by Og Mandino "The Greatest Salesman in the World". When I first saw the book I thought it was a nice gesture, but how can that help with bulimia? As I read the book over and over as instructed to do, it started to sink in that I am so much more powerful than I thought I was. I understand now why you were asked to read it over and over. It was a Good kind of brainwashing. You might think brainwashing is bad, but we do that to ourselves all the time. We tell ourselves bad stuff about ourselves, all the time. Is that not a negative way of brainwashing ourselves? Why is it so easy to criticize ourselves, but not praise? We are our own worst critic. We really shouldn't care what other people think because they are not nearly as hard on us as we are on ourselves.

CHAPTER 4

※

THE PROCESS......

*A*rmed with my new found sense of self (this was only the beginning), and my support system, I began working on my eating disorder. Of course like anyone else, I tried to tackle the issue all at once. I started watching what I ate, and trying to eat healthy. I really had to learn what that looked like. All my life I had either eaten what I wanted, or I was on a diet. There was really no in between. Back then I didn't have the benefit of the internet, so I read books and magazines to try to find out. There wasn't as much out there then, as there is now, but I found enough. Breakfast was easy, because I had a limited amount of time to get ready in the morning, and I really couldn't fudge. To help me along this process, I got up early in the morning to go to the gym before work. I only had a problem with breakfast when someone brought something like donuts or greasy biscuit to the office and also on weekends. I tried to conquer all the meals of the day, and I failed miserably. I would get so frustrated I wanted to give up so many times. Now I had people watching me, and available to kick my butt if I didn't keep trying, I couldn't give up. What I eventually did was to deal with one meal at a time, and forgive myself when I would mess up. The key is to keep trying not to mess up. What I'm telling you now is how I physically stop having bulimia. Later I will tell you how I received a complete cure.

It took me a very long time to master every meal. It was almost a year. I just did one meal at a time. Once I mastered breakfast, I moved on to lunch. Dinner was the most difficult since I was home and had access to that "Devil in the Kitchen". I decided that the best way to deal with that was to keep busy. I started going to the gym at night as well as in the morning. You might think "Oh, now she's addicted to exercise", and that is certainly a valid concern. The good news is that I was now at an acceptable weight. In fact, in order not to get overweight, and start all over again, I had to work out a lot. I had slowed down my metabolism so much with my bulimia; I would have gained weight just by eating normal. The exercise helped to speed up my metabolism, and kept me in great shape. My metabolism eventually got back to normal, and it will do the same for you, if you continue to eat correctly. It's funny that by having this problem, I learned how to eat healthy, and got on an exercise program at an early age.

I had gotten to a point where I did not throw up but once in awhile. It usually only happened when I got very stressed out. I had developed an emotional connection to food during the constant bulimia, and eating caused me to relax when I was stressed out. When I ate to relax, I would eat too much and then I would feel the need to throw. The good news is this seldom happened. I really didn't like the fact that it happened at all. Even if I used eating to relax, I should know when to stop. The truth of the matter is that I should not have been using eating to relax, or for any emotional outlet. Although I wasn't throwing up very often, I wasn't completely cured. I didn't know this at the time, so I began to focus on other issues that needed taking care of.

CHAPTER 5

THE MOVE......

$\mathcal{I}$ decided that since I was able to stop bulimia without any professional help, I was ready for bigger and better things. When I had gotten out of college, the economy was in terrible shape in Louisiana. The only job I could find was a Receptionist/New Accounts Clerk at a brokerage firm. Since I was not accustom to making a great deal of money, and since I had my "little problem", I was just happy to have money coming in. After conquering my eating disorder (for the most part), I felt very powerful. I felt like there was nothing I couldn't do if I put my mind to it.

The economy in Louisiana was not getting any better, and I was no longer content with my current pay and position, especially after four years of college. I decided that I needed a new location, and a new start. I started saving money in order to move, and started considering my options. I had two brothers who had moved away from Louisiana because of the economy. My brother Barry and his family had moved to Jacksonville Florida, and Keith and his family to Atlanta Georgia. I decided to visit Barry first since I liked the idea of a beach nearby. He and his family had moved into an apartment since they were not yet in financial shape to build a house. I went with my parents for visit, but we spent most of the time hanging out at their apartment. I didn't get to see much of Jacksonville, and therefore was not as interested as I might have been. The following year in April, my parents and I went to visit Keith. I took copies of my resume' up to Atlanta in hopes of finding work. I didn't find a job, but Keith, always the salesman, took us to see all the sights in Atlanta. Because I got a taste of the excitement of the city, I decided that Atlanta was the place for me.

At twenty five years old, I was moving to a place six hundred miles away from my parents. I had only been a maximum of seven miles away from them at my apartment in Lafayette. My brothers both had family and spouses, but I was moving alone. For some strange reason, I wasn't afraid. Since my search for a job on my earlier visit was unsuccessful, I didn't even have that going for me, but for some reason, I knew that everything would be fine. In fact I knew that this was exactly what I had to do. I also knew one other thing. If I could get my bulimia under control without the help of professionals and clinics, where so many others had failed, then I could do anything.

In August of 1987, I packed up everything I owned, and with enough money to live for one month, I moved to Atlanta. I even signed a twelve month lease. My Mother insisted on staying with me until I found a job. I wasn't going to argue with her about this. I was afraid to drive in this city because it was so big, so it was very nice not to have to stay alone at night for the first month. I had moved into my own place rather than stay with my brother. I have a very strong love of animals, and at the time I had three cats, and they were like children to me. My brother was not big on animals in the house, so it was out of the question that they would be welcome. That was ok because having all of my own stuff with me made me feel more at home in this big, strange city.

After two weeks I got a job offer at a brokerage firm, since that's where my previous experience was. I had figured out how much I needed to live on, and even with bare minimum, the salary was way too low. I told them that I could not accept anything less than $18,500. That's not too much to ask for a college graduate, in fact that is ridiculously low, but they were not prepared at that time to up the offer. I said NO! Somewhere deep down inside I knew that everything would be ok. I knew that what I needed would come to me, and I would be just fine. I got down to about one week's worth of money left, and the company called back and increased their offer. I got what I asked for. I had another "knowing" in that experience, and I trusted it. I still don't know why I knew, or what was going on, but I trusted that everything would be ok, and it was. I was on my way to healing and growth, even thought I didn't realize it at the time.

My Mom went home, and I started my job, still expecting that I may have some difficulty adjusting, but I would be ok. I figured that I might be a little lonely for awhile, but I was willing to accept that in exchange for a new life and a new start. A Brand New Life!

CHAPTER 6

CLOSE ENCOUNTERS OF THE SPIRITUAL KIND....

*B*efore I move on, I want to make it clear that what you will be reading next is not an endorsement of any particular religion or belief. I am simply relating my experiences on the road to healing. Every person can come to the end result of "Healing" without participation in any religious belief. I just found it easier this way. This was my path, and you may be on a different road than I. As long as you take the action that I took to heal myself, than you don't have to walk in my shoes to get there.

I was Catholic at the time, so my brother suggested I join the singles group at the Church nearby. I thought it was a pretty good idea since they met on Sunday night right after church. I attended the first meeting, and found out they had a social calendar with other activities besides Sunday night. This was great because not only was I not lonely, but I had more things to do than I did in Louisiana. I didn't even have to plan anything, it was done for me. All I had to do was show up.

Life in this new city was pretty good. I was having fun, and even though I still didn't have that great of a job, I was happy. To offset the lack of accomplishment in my work, I started training for a Triathlon. I finished the Triathlon, and shortly after landed a job in sales that paid somewhat better than the brokerage firm. I was making progress in the material world, but my real progress and growth was soon to come.

The church was starting a youth group, and the singles group was asked for volunteers to be youth leaders. I liked doing charitable work, so I was happy to help out. Not long after I started working with the youths, I met a girl who was friends with the Youth Minister. She invited me to attend a retreat. I had been on retreats when I was a kid, and always enjoyed them, so I said yes. Little did I know that this weekend would change my life forever!

I had always had a desire for a closer relationship with God. When I was young I wanted to go to church and on retreats. I had "Given my life to Christ", at a very young age. I loved anything spiritual. I also remember trying to meditate at a very young age. So you see, I had a fascination with anything that was spiritual, but I also had a fascination with anything that seemed supernatural too. I wrote a paper on Voodoo in the eighth grade because I lived in Louisiana, and New Orleans was full of stories of Voodoo and magic. They even had a Voodoo Museum which I attended with glee. Then in college I wrote a paper on Parapsychology, and I even tried some of the exercises, and was hoping to find out if I was psychic. I just knew there was more out there than what meets the eye. On this retreat I would experience for the first time a direct, personal encounter with God, or "The Source".

The retreat was fun and informative, and everything was pretty much what I expected until we were asked to go to confession. We were supposed to reflect on our life for awhile, and when we were ready, go to confession. I had been baptized Catholic, and except for a few years of going to the Methodist religion, I had been Catholic. Somehow I had been able to escape going to confession. I didn't really believe that someone else could forgive your sins, so I couldn't bring myself to go through the humiliation of bearing my soul to another person for nothing. I didn't really plan to go to confession on the retreat, but as I sat there thinking about my life, I started to change my mind. There were things that I regretted doing, things that I felt bad about, and that felt unfinished in my mind. Suddenly as I sat there I felt like I was getting lighter physically. I started having this weird sensation that if I didn't get up and go to confession, then I would start levitating. I was so worried that I would have to explain why my body was floating in the air; I got over the mortification of confession, and got in line to see the priest. The confession itself was uneventful, but the wonderful feeling of relief after confession was amazing. I don't really think confession is about someone else forgiving us, it's about forgiving ourselves. That's not how it's set up in the Church, but that was the end result, at least in my case. I've since then learned that dwelling on past experiences and guilt are a waste of energy. You can only live in the now, and guilt doesn't fix anything. All you can do is try your best to make amends and move forward.

I had another strange experience that night. There was a ritual called "Baptism in the Spirit". In this event the retreat team, as well as other guest, pray over you as a group. This is not ordinary prayer; this is prayer in "Tongues". During the retreat we learned that there are many "Gifts of the Spirit". One of these gifts is the "Gift of

Tongues". In this gift you are given an Angelic language which is understood by God, and is used even when you are uncertain what the person you are praying for needs. If you haven't guessed by now, this was not a standard Catholic retreat. It was a Catholic Charismatic retreat. I had never realized that there was such a thing in the Catholic Church until that point in time. I had heard whispered that some of the singles were involved in some kind of strange prayer group, but no one really knew what went on there. This group believed that different people received different gifts to use to move closer to God, and help others in the world. What I have since learned is that all the gifts they discussed were indeed available to us, but all of the gifts, not just one or two. Jesus said in the Bible, "That even the least among you can do all these things, and even greater". I'm not sure why so many churches pass right over this like it's no big deal. In my opinion, this is one of the most exciting messages in the Bible. I've always been blown away by this, and wanted to know more about it. I have friends in some religions that could recite all of the Old Testament to you, but had never heard of that passage. It's almost like it's too special and empowering to let the congregation know about. What's up with that?

The night of the Baptism was here. I was so excited. Since I had learned about the Gifts of the Spirit, I was fired up. Considering my love of the supernatural, this stuff was way cool. I was told that during the time they were praying over me, I might receive a gift. I was totally pumped up, but I was determined that I would not "make" something happen just to say that it did.

My turn came, and they started praying over me, and it sounded just like you would imagine Angels would sound. I cleared my mind and relaxed into the moment. I started feeling a lifting again, but this time it was different. The last time I felt like I was being pushed to get up, this time I felt like angelic hands were lifting me up like people do when they present a baby at Baptism. I started getting a tickle in the back of my throat. I was so determined to not fake anything that I was fighting it. My tongue wanted to move, but I wouldn't let it. I wasn't afraid; I just wanted it to be the real deal. The tickling got stronger and I finally had to let it go. My tongue started moving and this weird jibber jabber came out that was no words that I had ever heard. It seemed to be a short little phrase, and it kept repeating over and over like I was being taught. I finally gave in and consciously started repeating the phrase on my own, Oh My God; I had just received the gift of tongues. Was this for real? I knew it was because I had no clue where this came from. I was so happy that I received this gift that I was blown away.

The next day, the priest topped off my weekend by saying, "She is so special" while he was anointing my head with oil. He said it like he was having a discussion with God. It was so cool because he said it about me, not to me. I have to say that was one weekend that I felt my heart would burst from the amount of Love that was sent to and from it. That was definitely one of the best weekends of my life. I learned so much more since that weekend about who we really are, and how life works, but that weekend was a pivotal point in my life, and I would never be the same from that point forward. I had a direct experience of the Creator, not just learning about him. Once you get that close, you are never satisfied with knowing Him from a distance.

During my involvement with this Prayer Group, a very powerful experience happened. I would help out on the "Team" whenever we had a retreat. I started experiencing great sadness while helping people attending the retreat. I thought it was just my experiencing the emotional pain of the attendees. This kind of empathy is not uncommon when you're trying to help people through painful times. The problem is that my pain was constant during the retreat, and too strong and real to be an experience of empathy.

On one retreat, one of my team members pulled me aside and explained this to me. She said that what I was experiencing had to be my own pain to be that intense. She offered to help me out, and I accepted. She asked me to close my eyes and try to remember back to something in my childhood that was extremely painful. I assumed she was talking about my parents, and I told her that I was very fortunate to have great patents. The more I thought about it, I started to remember the neighborhood where I suffered so much hurt, pain, and torment from the neighborhood kids. I was the youngest girl, and I went home crying every night because of their taunting and teasing. I remembered how much my Grandmother had hurt me and made me feel inferior while I was growing up, and I also remembered my brother who had sent me the letter. When I was growing up, he tortured my sister by constantly picking on her. As I got older, he started doing the same thing to me. That's why I thought he hated me. I thought I was past all that, but as I remembered the events, the pain felt equally as real. I know now if I had been over those experiences, I would have felt no pain associated with the events.

My friend asked me to think of all the people that had hurt me so badly during that time. She asked me to picture them in my mind like I was there with them now. I saw all of the people who had caused me continuous emotional pain, and the hurt felt very intense and real. I started crying, but I tried to focus on what she wanted me to do. She then asked me to walk over to each of them, give them a hug, and tell them that I forgive them. The pain was so great at that point that I just wanted it to end. One by one, I went to each person and told them that I forgave them and that I loved them. Every time I did this the pain lessened till there was nothing left. By this time I was sobbing. She then asked me to see myself as I was then. She said for me, the adult, to go to me, the child and tell her that I loved her too. She told me to tell my inner child that I would take care of her and never let anyone hurt her that way again. I did what she said, and an amazing peace came over me. I felt very safe and secure. I trusted myself as an adult to make good on that promise. She told me to picture a playground where Jesus and I could play. I remembered a park that was by my house when I was very young. It had a manual "Merry Go Round" where someone pushed it round and round, while someone else road the ride. I saw myself on the "Merry Go Round", and Jesus was pushing it round and round so that I could enjoy the ride. By this time I was laughing and crying for joy at the same time. It was truly an amazing experience. The most amazing experience of all happened after that.

I told you earlier in the book that although I controlled my Bulimia, it was by shear will alone. I also told you that my real healing came later. This is when I was finally healed completely of the Bulimia. Although I had not been practicing Bulimia, It still felt like something I had to control, especially when I was stressed out. After this experience of forgiveness, I no longer felt the desire again. I'm telling you this because I believe this can work for any kind of addiction. Like I said before, more problems are a result of a hurt that has not been healed or resolved. The easiest way to heal and resolve a hurt is to forgive the person who has hurt you. It's not forgiveness for their sake; it's for your sake. The person who truly benefits from forgiveness is the one doing the forgiving. In most cases the one who is forgiven doesn't even know what's going on.

Forgiveness is a very powerful and healing gift that is available to all of us. Don't let your Ego get in the way of your healing, and moving on with your life. The only one that will suffer from that is you. To me, this is one of the most powerful and amazing things I have learned in my life. It's so simple, yet it's almost like very few people are aware of it's awesome power. This is one of the most truly miraculous gifts.

I continued in that Prayer Group for quite some time. I finally left when I started stumbling upon information of enlightenment. Book by book would make its way to me, and I began to realize more and more that there was information that I needed to know. I was beginning to suspect that I might not find it in the Church, but for now that was all I had. I continued going to regular churches for awhile till I felt like I was hearing the same thing over and over. I didn't want to just "go through the motions"; I wanted to learn something new. My opportunity was quite a few years later. I had to go through some of the everyday lessons before I would be ready to experience more miracles. God, The Source, The Zone, The Alpha and The Omega, or whatever you call the powerful force that created everything, is very much a Gentleman. He or She doesn't give you anything you're not ready for.

CHAPTER 7

THE NEVER ENDING JOURNEY....

I hope you will use what I have shared with you to resolve some of your own issues. Forgiveness is the key to your own happy life, no matter how painful of an experience you have gone through. In fact, the more painful, the more necessary forgiveness becomes. Forgiving yourself is equally as important as forgiving someone else. Like I said before, we are our own worst critic. No one else can be as hard on us as we are on ourselves. Even if you do have someone who is always very critical of you, the only reason they can affect you is that you are buying into what they are saying. No one deserves forgiveness as much as you do. Stop beating yourself up, and stop holding resentment for past hurts. I'm not asking you to keep someone toxic in your life, quite the contrary. I'm asking you to let them go by forgiving them. Until you forgive them, they will always have a hold over you. You also will continue to relive the bad experience over and over again. It was bad enough that it happened to you the first time, but you are the one who makes it happen again and again after that.

Some of you may have stuffed the bad experiences so far down that you can't remember them. Find someone that you trust, and ask them to be with you while you try to remember the pain. It may take a very long time, but keep trying. If you have an obsessive behavior, then there is something down there that needs forgiveness. If you can't remember on your own, you may have to seek help. Hypnosis can help bring up buried experiences that are so painful that you can only access them from the subconscious level. Those experiences need to be acknowledged and forgiven.

One thing I need to make clear is that although I have resolved all those childhood hurts, it doesn't mean that now I am immune to recent painful events. Sometimes you will get hit with even bigger things than those from your childhood. The good news is that every time you move beyond these events, you get a little stronger. Like I said, God is a gentleman. He doesn't give you anything bigger than you can handle.

I still have to remind myself about forgiveness in the little day to day hurts as well. Those little hurts can add up and create a big pain in your heart. Let it go. Forgive the person, and send them on their way, if need be. One thing we all need to learn is to let go of toxic people. You should try to love everyone, but that doesn't mean you have to like them, or have them in your life. Surround yourself with healthy loving friends and family. I know you can't always choose who is around you on a daily basis. There will be times when you are forced to be around someone who is hurtful and toxic because you work with them, or they are a family member. Just make sure you don't buy into the hurtful things they say. Forgive them for the pain they cause you, even if you have to do this every single day. Remember, forgiveness is for you, not for them. Then try your best to send them your love, from a distance if at all possible. What may help you is to remember that they weren't born a mean person. Someone or something hurt them badly, and they have not yet learned how to deal with the pain, so they strike out at others. They probably hate themselves after that, so they have even more damage to their psyche. They haven't learned the power of forgiveness, so they live in pain. This can help you to have a little compassion for their addiction to hurting people.

Start practicing forgiveness today. Think of how you feel about the people you deal with on a daily basis. If you have any bad feelings, then there is probably something to forgive. By the same token, think about how you feel about yourself. If you feel bad about yourself, then it's time to look in the mirror and say, "Hey Beautiful (because YOU are Beautiful), I know you have made some mistakes. I know you have screwed up at one time or another. I know you don't think you are all that you could be. But guess what? I forgive you! I love you! And you are the most special person in the world to me" Be proactive, and don't wait for a problem to develop before you decide to get your "Forgiveness On". It's like taking out the garbage. If you don't take the garbage out on a regular basis to be picked up and discarded, then it's going start stinking really badly.

CHAPTER 8

※

THE WORK....

*O*ne thing I want to make clear to you is that getting over your eating disorder is going to be work. I know this is a very small book, so I don't want you to think that you can just read this book, do a little "forgiveness work", and "BOOM", you're over your Bulimia. You didn't develop this eating disorder overnight, and it's not likely you will be cured overnight. It's going to be hard work, and the longer you have had this problem, the harder the process. The thing to remember is that, anything worthwhile is probably going to be some work. Getting over your eating disorder is not only worthwhile; it is "Life Changing".

If I had to do it over again, I would start with the Forgiveness first. I did it backwards because I didn't know at the time what forgiveness can do. Working on forgiving all the hurts and pain from your past, and the people who caused them, along with forgiving yourself (don't forget the most important person), will make the process much easier.

After you have done your "Forgiveness Work", the rest is dealing with the "Bad Habit" that you have developed. Like any bad habit, it's going to take time to get over.

The first step is to understand what healthy eating looks like. You are much more fortunate than me because you have the internet. You can find an unlimited amount of information at your fingertips.

Believe it or not, healthy eating does not mean sacrificing taste. There are thousands of things you can eat that actually taste good. I'm not talking about a diet. The problem with dieting is that the minute you go back to eating the way you did before, you gain weight. What I'm talking about is changing the way you eat on a regular basis. Make most of your meals something healthy, but tasty. I was a personal trainer at one point in my life, and I always told my clients, "If you eat healthy all week long, then reward yourself with one meal a week. Eat something you love, and would consider a "No No" on that one meal so you don't feel deprived. This is especially important when you are totally changing the way you eat.

Binge eaters are going to have the biggest problem because you have stretched your stomach. You are going to have to reduce your amount of food to something closer to normal. Because your stomach is stretched, you are going to feel hungry, at least in the beginning. Try drinking a lot of water to help you feel full. Adding a little lemon will help curb your appetite some. When you have a meal, be sure to eat protein because it will make you feel satisfied longer. The good news is that your internal stomach can shrink back pretty quickly.

People with anorexia and bulimia have not stretched their stomach, but your task is the same as binge eaters. Learn what eating healthy looks like. Find healthy food that you feel can satisfy you on a regular basis. Take one meal at a time and conquer it, then move on to the next. Forgive yourself when you slip, and reward yourself when you make it a whole week in your new lifestyle.

Another little tip I would like to share with you about eating. Every time you put something in your mouth, be aware of why you are eating. Are you really hungry? Is this the best food I can feed myself? Am I going to be better for eating this, or worse? What is the purpose of food? Thinking about why you are eating will help you to not just eat out of boredom, habit, or for emotional benefit. Remember, food is there to help you maintain life, not to become your life. If you have trouble with this, put little reminders around you house. Make a big sign in bold red letters, with the word THINK on it. Put that sign on every pantry, cabinet, and refrigerator that has food in it. After awhile this will come naturally, and you won't need the signs, but for now, use the signs to help you remember.

Now I'm going to say the dirty word, "EXERCISE". I know there are people out there who are allergic to exercise. I just want to make you aware of why this is important at this point in time.

People who have binge eating disorder, I have good news for you. Because you haven't been starving yourself, you haven't caused your metabolism to slow down. Exercise is important to you for your health, to burn calories, and it can also speed up your metabolism.

For those of you with anorexia and bulimia, you are likely to have a metabolism that is greatly reduced. On your journey to healthy eating, it would be very beneficial for you to start an exercise program, if you don't have one already. I'm not talking about running a marathon, or doing a triathlon. Just like eating, find an exercise that you can enjoy a little, and do it. One thing you might want to consider is weight training. You don't have to get really big and muscular for this to benefit you. It takes a lot more calories to maintain muscle than fat. The more muscular your body is, the more calories you will burn just sitting on the couch. Cardiovascular exercise is great for your heart, and important too because it burns calories. I would suggest a combination of both if you want to see the best results, and get through this easier.

Forgiveness at this point is more important than ever. You may slip up, and when you do, forgive yourself, and keep on trying. I promise that if you keep trying, and forgiving, you can, and will overcome your obsession with food. The more you do this, the more you will break the emotional ties that you have developed with food. You created those emotional ties, and you can break them.

I want you to do one more thing as you go through this process. I want you to imagine how you will feel when you have successfully conquered your eating disorder. I want you to do this every morning when you wake up, and every night before you go to bed.

You eat only when you're hungry, and eat mostly healthy food. You are exercising, and becoming more muscular. You have so much more energy because the foods you are eating are rich in vitamins and nutrients, and exercising has increased your energy and vitality. You enjoy your food, but you don't live for your food. In fact food is more like something you do to stay healthy. You want your body to be healthy because your body is your vehicle that you use to access your "True Self" in this world. You love yourself and you know that you deserve the best, so you are going to take the best care of you.

You have regained control of your life, and you are overcoming great obstacles. You are a Very Powerful Being, and this is only the beginning. This is just a stepping stone to the Wonderful New Life that you are creating for yourself. There is nothing you can't do if you put your mind to it. There is nothing you can't be. You are in Control, and you are Healed, Healthy, and truly Amazing!

Printed in the United States
By Bookmasters